WALKS IN THE COTSWOLDS

Walks in
The Cotswolds

R. HODGES

To my parents

SPURBOOKS LIMITED

Published by
SPURBOOKS LIMITED
6 Parade Court
Bourne End
Buckinghamshire

© SPURBOOKS LIMITED 1976

Sketch Maps by MIKE POCOCK

ISBN 0 904978 13 3

Printed by Maund & Irvine, Tring, Herts.

Contents

Walks in the South Cotswolds

Introduction

These walks attempt to include all the attractive types of landscape in the Cotswolds: the scarp, the combes, the valleys, and the extensive high fields across the top. It is this variety that makes the Cotswolds such pleasant and stimulating countryside in which to walk. However, it is sad to admit that some of these paths have not been well walked in recent years. One cause of this was the change from sheep-farming to arable farming during the middle years of this century. Many of the paths which once crossed open hillsides now lead across large ploughed expanses. With this problem in mind I have chosen to follow the lanes where possible as alternatives to paths across cornfields. However, some ploughed fields are inevitably part of some of these walks and walkers are asked to skirt them, to respect the crops, except of course where there is stubble. Nevertheless, at certain times of the year ploughed fields can be most unpleasant so I have included some walks which mostly follow the lanes and which link monuments or areas of particular interest.

The sheep economy was the basis of the prehistoric, Roman and medieval wealth of the Cotswolds. This wealth has been crystallized in a series of fine monuments of all these periods which many of these walks visit or pass. The Neolithic barrows of Nympsfield, The Camp and Daglingworth, and the Iron Age fortresses of Uleybury and Old Sodbury are some typical examples of the prehistoric wealth acquired from sheep farming the Cotswolds; this same wealth that enabled a rich Roman to build the very fine villa at Chedworth. Cotswold sheep were one of the famous breeds of the medieval world. The extraordinarily wealthy medieval wool-merchants have left their mark in the elegant country churches and most notably in the famous tower of Gloucester Cathedral visible from many of these walks. One of the other great monuments in the Cotswolds is the canal that climbs up from the Severn to join the Thames, and passes through a tunnel two miles long cut through the hill beneath Sapperton. This was built in the late 18th century and used until early this century.

The Cotswolds are rich with history and there is the sense of a lost age wherever you go. It is excellent walking country; both peaceful and picturesque. There are good centres to use as a base, like Bath, Stroud, Cirencester, Gloucester, Cheltenham and even Oxford. It is, of course, easier if you have your own transport, but a number of buses from all these towns visit the villages and hamlets. There are pleasant unpretentious pubs and occasionally some really good tea-shops. Finally, always obey the country code, and ask farmers whenever you are in doubt.

RICHARD HODGES

Walk 1

Broadway—Broadway Tower—Saintbury
4 and 7 miles

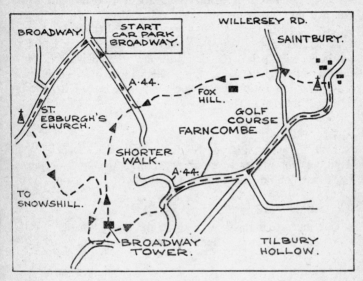

THIS is an easy long walk which includes the famous Broadway Tower. From the Tower there is a marvellous view across the rich Vale of Evesham. It is an excellent place to picnic, to sit (seats provided) and to meditate. The walk also passes two fine medieval churches; St. Ebburgh's, the first church to be built at Broadway, and Saintbury church which has a fine steeple.

How to get there: Broadway is a small town on the A44; it lies at the foot of the Cotswold escarpment about six miles south-east of Evesham.

By bus: Contact **Castleways Ltd.,** 72 Crispin Road, Winchcombe, for details.

Parking: At the west end of the village is a large car park with toilets.

Refreshments: Teas, ices, etc., at Broadway Tower; in Broadway itself there are pubs, restaurants and cafes.

Opposite the car-park at the west end of the village is the turning to Snowshill. Follow this road as far as St. Ebburgh's church, a distance of about ¾ of a mile. The route from here is up the medieval road on your left (signposted) towards Broadway Tower. This is Conygree Lane: fork left after 400 yards, and turn left after a further 400 yards. The path then climbs up through the fields to the lane on the top. It is a steep climb which must have made past travellers puff furiously. At the road turn left to Broadway Tower (entry 15p).

4 mile walk

Take the path which descends the scarp directly below the Tower (signposted). After about a mile it comes out in a back lane behind Broadway High Street.

To continue 7 mile walk

Continue from the Tower along the scarp top signposted: Cotswold Way), and after ½ a mile you descend about a hundred feet through a beech copse to the A44. Follow the road down the hill for about 100 yards and then turn right (be extremely careful, this is a busy road). This little lane climbs up the scarp face (ignore the turning on your left to Farncombe) to a cross-roads. Here take the Saintbury road to your left down past a golf course. The village of Saintbury is about a mile away perched on the side of the hill. The path back to Broadway begins by the entrance to the church. It crosses two fields interconnected by a stile, before reaching the Willersey road. Take the Fox Hill lane directly opposite and follow it ¼ of a mile **past** the main entrance of the first house on the right; the second entrance to this house is a small gate. The path now actually goes through this gate, around the garden, over a stile in the far fence and on down through the fields to the lane that leads into Broadway. (It is prudent to ask permission at this house before following the path around their garden.) From this house to Broadway it

10

is a distance of about a mile. The lane comes out on the A44 at the far end of the town, so it is a further short walk back to the car-park past the shops etc.

Walk 2

Hailes—Farmcote—Winchcombe
3¼ and 5 miles

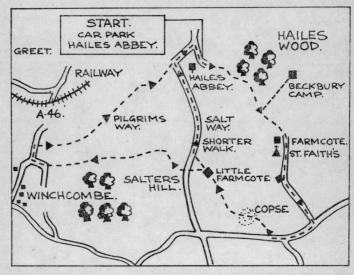

THIS walk begins at Hailes Abbey founded by Prince Richard of Cornwall in the thirteenth century as a result of an oath he took when his ship was floundering in the Mediterranean. (It is now a scheduled monument and is open throughout the year.) The path climbs up around the combe passing the Saxon chapel at Farmcote, and coming down to Winchcombe. The last section follows the route the pilgrims once took to Hailes.

How to get there: Hailes Abbey is well signposted. It lies a mile east of the A46 (by road) 3 miles north of Winchcombe. By bus: Contact **Castleways Ltd.,** 72 Crispin Road, Winchcombe for details.
There is a large car park opposite the abbey.

Refreshments: Teashops and pubs in Winchcombe.

Follow the road up the hill, past the abbey. After $\frac{1}{2}$ a mile the surfaced lane bears right into a fruit farm; on the left is a track which goes straight up the hill through hazel woods. The climb is steep until the track emerges from the wood on to the top. At this point on your left is the path to Beckbury hillfort (signposted) which is worth visiting though you must return to the track to continue this walk. The track leads on to Farmcote, an elegant farm perched on the edge of the scarp. Just beyond the farm is St. Faith's chapel which has a blocked Saxon chancel arch, and a fine north facing Saxon window as well as a well preserved medieval timber roof. The lane continues for $\frac{3}{4}$ of a mile around the combe until it meets the Winchcombe lane. Turn right at this junction and after 300 yards is another junction at which you keep straight on. Just past this second junction, on the right, is a gate. The path from this gate follows the side of the hill to a gate in a copse (visible from the first gate). Go through the copse and continue around the hillside for $\frac{1}{4}$ of a mile to Little Farmcote.

$3\frac{1}{4}$ mile walk

Just beyond Little Farmcote take the lane (right) down the hill. This is the Salt Way and it leads directly to Hailes in the combe.

To continue 5 mile walk

The main walk continues from the farm along the upper track 50 yards to the Hailes lane, the Salt Way. Directly opposite is a gate and the path to Winchcombe. The path goes straight on until you are on the end of the spur. Here turn left and continue on this contour about 50 yards to a wicket gate. Bear down across the next field, which is a rough pasture, for 300 yards keeping above the woods. When you reach a stone walled sheep pen there is a track running down the slope to your right. Follow the track down the hill; after $\frac{1}{2}$ a mile it reaches a fenced field (with gates at the top and bottom ends) which you must cross. Beyond this field is a track which leads down to the A46. If you turn left along the main road you will arrive at Winchcombe after $\frac{1}{2}$ a mile. It is a very attractive little town with tea-shops, restaurants, bookshops etc.

To return to Hailes turn right along the main road for 50 yards, then take the first turning to your right. At the end of the surfaced lane is a track which in turn becomes a foot-path. This is the Pilgrim's Way to Hailes and the path through the fields is well indicated by signs and yellow blobs. Beyond the fields is the Salt Way which you follow (to your left) 200 yards to Hailes.

Walk 3

Bourton on the Hill—Sezincote—Longborough
4½ miles

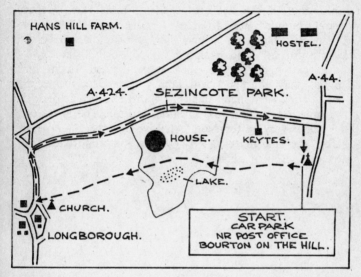

THIS is an easy walk through Sezincote Park, returning along the top of a wold from where there is an excellent view. Sezincote is an exotic looking mansion which was remodelled in 1805 by Sir Charles Cockerell of the East India Company. The same style was incorporated in Brighton pavilion built a decade after Sezincote.

How to get there: Bourton on the hill is on the A44.
By bus: Contact **Pulham & Sons Ltd.**, Station Road Garage, Bourton-on-the-Water.
Park near the Post Office to the south of the main road.

Refreshments: There are several pubs and restaurants in Bourton. In Longborough there is the **Coach and Horses** which has a garden.

Take the grass track which begins directly behind the church and leads out into the fields. It is a simple route, for the path through the pasture, copses and grounds of Sezincote Park, is well served with gates and stiles. Keeping straight ahead you will arrive at Sezincote Park after about $\frac{1}{2}$ a mile. There, keep above the lake and head for the stile in the far top corner of the field below the great house. Continue straight on and after two miles the path skirts the graveyard of Longborough church, and then reaches the village. The early fourteenth century church is well worth visiting.

Leave Longborough by the Candicote road which climbs up the scarp through open country to a junction $\frac{1}{2}$ a mile away. Turn right here and follow the lane back along the two mile edge of the wold towards Bourton. The view across the vale is very pastoral and extensive. In a beech copse, just before the lane meets the A44, there is a well-trodden path down into Bourton village.

Walk 4

Lower Slaughter—Lower Swell—Upper Slaughter
3¼ and 4½ miles

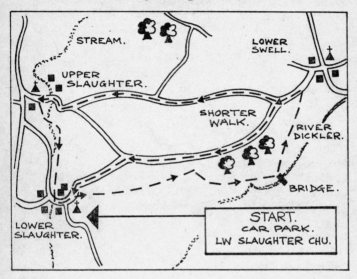

THE Slaughter villages are some of the prettiest in the Cotswolds. They lie in a verdant valley that is perfectly tranquil. These two walks are very easy.

How to get there: The Slaughter villages are situated between the A436 and A429 3 miles south of Stow on the Wold.
By bus: Contact **Pulham & Sons Ltd.,** Station Road Garage, Bourton-on-the-Water.
Park by Lower Slaughter church.

Refreshments: The mill in Lower Slaughter is a post office and sells confectionery and ices.

At 100 yards beyond the church on the Lower Swell road there is a pathway (signposted) on your right. The path leads through the meadows and is signposted all the way. After nearly a mile there is a footpath junction in the centre of a field (you will see signposts in three hedgerows pointing at you). Turn to your right in the direction of Hyde mill. The path goes diagonally across the fields to the little river Dickler which is lined with willows. The Hyde mill path crosses a bridge after having followed the river for about 300 yards. Your path, however, continues along the left bank, following a tributary to a gate 200 yards from the bridge in the corner of the field. Afterwards the path climbs up a gentle slope, skirting a fenced copse, and continues across the fields away from the valley to a lane which leads to Lower Swell.

Lower Swell is a pretty little village, and from it footpaths run northwards following the valley.

To return to the Slaughter villages, take the signposted lane. In fact, the lane which led out of the valley to Lower Swell first meets the Slaughter road. After $\frac{1}{2}$ a mile along this road, which leads towards both Lower and Upper Slaughter, the path forks to left and right.

$3\frac{1}{4}$ mile walk

Fork left at this junction and follow the lane along the lower slope of the hill back to Lower Slaughter village.

To continue $4\frac{1}{2}$ mile walk

For the slightly longer route, take the right fork, following the lane which crosses the hilltop and then descends into the valley and the village of Upper Slaughter through a lovely avenue of trees. The village is actually situated several hundred yards beyond the little river which the lane crosses after leaving the trees. The path back to Lower Slaughter begins on your left 50 yards after the river, and before you reach the centre of the village. The path through the meadows is well marked and served with stiles, and after $\frac{3}{4}$ of a mile it brings you out by the famous mill, now a post office, at Lower Slaughter.

Walk 5

Sherborne—Great Barrington—Little Barrington—Windrush
6 miles

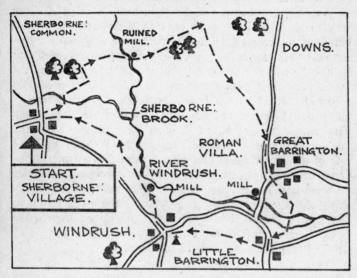

THIS walk crosses the farmland between several picturesque villages. It is an easy walk only in the autumn after the corn has been harvested. Many of these paths cross the centres of large fields which, at other times of the year, it is prudent to skirt around.

How to get there: Sherborne lies a mile north of the A40, half-way between Northleach and Burford.
By bus: Contact **R. S. Marchant,** 433 High Street, Cheltenham.
There is parking space in the village by the side of the road.

Refreshments: There are none along the way.

THE walk begins off Clapton lane, situated at the east end of Sherborne. The path is signposted and goes to the left of a row of cottages. Behind the cottages is a track; turn left and follow this track to Sherborne brook about 200 yards from the stile. The walk continues across two fields to a track on the far side of the second field. The path, however, is not clear so after crossing the brook bear out across the first field to your right, making for the right-hand edge of a copse which runs along part of the far side of this field. There is a gate into the second field and the path turns diagonally across the field to the far corner; however the field is often ploughed so it is best to follow the edge of the field to a gate by the track. Turn right along the track and follow it to a stream by a ruined mill. The track now turns to the left and begins to climb the slope and then disappears into a very large field. The way is straight ahead through this and the next field, keeping to the left of a large copse which is on the right-hand side of the second field. You enter a third field as soon as the copse on your right ends. Cross this field keeping the hedge on your **left**. Beyond the hedge that forms the east side of this field, directly in front of you, is the path to Great Barrington. (These three fields from the ruined mill to the Great Barrington path are usually ploughed. It is slow going uphill, **straight ahead** for about $\frac{3}{4}$ of a mile).

There is a gate out of this third field, and the Great Barrington path is to your right. It follows the hedge down the hill then up again and is marked with red splashes all the way to the Great Barrington road $\frac{3}{4}$ of a mile away. Turn right down the road and at the cross-roads which you reach after 200 yards, bear slightly **left** and go straight over. This is a little lane which becomes a track that leads down to a mill by the Windrush river. You cross the river twice; first just beyond the mill (keeping straight on), and then at the far end of the next field. After the second bridge turn right down a clearly defined path that leads to the large green in Little Barrington.

Go across the green to the post office (signposted, and to the right of a farmyard). By the side of the post office is a pathway to a stile that leads out into the fields, towards Windrush. Bear slightly to your left across the grassed fields from stile to stile, keeping straight on for about $\frac{1}{2}$ a mile, before Windrush church comes into view. The path comes out onto the Sherborne lane by the church. The church itself is worth visiting, and it has a fine decorated twelfth century south doorway. Continue along the Sherborne lane for about 250 yards, then take a track on your right past some cottages which leads to the fields just above Windrush mill. The path continues to the south of the mill following the hedgerows across the slopes past a barn, and straight on for just over a mile to Sherborne. It meets the path behind the cottages where this walk first began. Again it is not easy to follow parts of the path from the mill to Sherborne because some of the fields are ploughed. Two points, therefore, should be stressed. First, make sure you are to the south of the mill and following the fields across the slopes, not following the River Windrush which veers to the north. Secondly, just beyond the barn Sherborne village comes into view and it is a good marker to follow when you skirt around the large ploughed fields.

Walk 6

Birdlip—Great Witcombe Roman Villa—Great Witcombe
5 miles

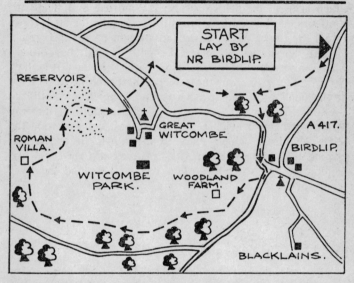

THIS walk makes a big circle inside one large combe overlooking Gloucester, with the Malverns beyond. You begin on the rough wold and pass through deciduous plantations down to the valley at Witcombe where there is a reservoir which attracts a large variety of water-birds. This walk also includes the little Roman Villa at Great Witcombe which is usually open to the public. As the poor relation of Chedworth Roman Villa, it is rather interesting.

How to get there: Birdlip is on the A417 about 6 miles from Gloucester.

By bus: Only the No. 555 passes through Birdlip on its way from Gloucester to Cirencester. There is a more frequent service, No. 584, from Gloucester to Witcombe and you could begin this circular walk at Witcombe.

Park in the large lay-by between the **Hot Air Balloon** and Birdlip.

Refreshments: The **King George** in Birdlip, and the **Hot Air Balloon** a mile in the direction of Gloucester from Birdlip on the A417.

This walk begins in the large lay-by between the **Hot Air Balloon** and Birdlip. The view from here is magnificent, and includes on your right Crickley Hill, an Iron Age fortress. The path leads along the side of the scarp through the rough called Barrow Wake, and then around the wooded spur called the Peak to the road $\frac{1}{2}$ a mile away which climbs up to Birdlip. Just before the village take the Stroud road on your right, the B4070, and then almost immediately take the signposted trackway on the right for Cooper's Hill. Follow this track for about a mile through the beech woods. Only after passing some ornamental gate-posts should you turn off, again to the right. This track leads down and around a small combe, and on the far side is the track, on your right, to Great Witcombe Roman Villa which is only about 300 yards away but will be concealed from you when you turn off. The villa is on your left as you emerge from the trees; the main path, however, follows the stream on your right about $\frac{1}{2}$ a mile down the valley to the reservoir. Here there is a track that at one point is a causeway dividing two reservoirs. Immediately the reservoir ends, 40 yards before a small farm, there is a crude stile on your right. Go over the stile and across two fields, linked by another stile, to Great Witcombe village. The path emerges onto the lane on the north side of the village which is just to your right. At this lane turn left for 20 yards, and then take the well-trodden pathway through the fields on your right. It is only about $\frac{1}{4}$ of a mile to the busy Birdlip road; cross straight over, with care, and for a 100 yards follow another path to a small lane. Turn right up the lane and continue up the path which brings you back at the Peak; beyond is the path for the **Hot Air Balloon.** This last stretch is scarcely a mile but with a thirst it seems like ten!

Walk 7

Edge—Haresfield Beacon—Randwick
3½, 4 or 6 miles

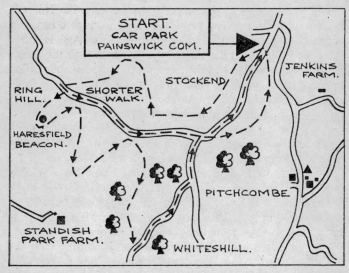

THIS is an easy walk along the escarpment. Much of it, in fact, follows the Cotswold Way and so it is well signposted. There are some superb views of the Severn Vale and Gloucester en route.

How to get there: Edge is on the B4072 between Pitchcombe and Gloucester, 3½ miles north of Stroud. In the village take the lane signposted to Randwick.

By bus: The No. 556 Gloucester–Nailsworth stops at Edge approximately every hour. From Randwick there is an infrequent service, the No. 441, to Stroud.

Park in the car park on the edge of Painswick Common, about 250 yards along the Randwick lane on the left.

Refreshments: The **Vine Tree** in Randwick.

About 100 yards along the Randwick road, having left the B4072, there is a lane on the right signposted to Stockend which passes down through the beech woods. After 250 yards fork left (in reality keep straight on) along a gravel track which climbs gradually to a house with a curious spire. Beyond this house there is only a pathway which follows the contours around the hillside through the wood and emerges after $\frac{1}{2}$ a mile at a surfaced lane. Go down the lane 300 yards then turn left, opposite Tump farm, to Haresfield Beacon (signposted). The path climbs around the scarp and there are spectacular views. It passes an inscription commemorating the 1645 siege of Gloucester, and continues on, becoming a track. The track comes out at Ring Hill. Here turn left up the hill and almost immediately climb the stile on the right and the path beyond which leads up to the little Iron Age promontory fortress of Haresfield Beacon. Follow the natural defences of the fortress to your right. At the far corner of the camp, by the trigonometry point there is a splendid view of the vale and the Severn Bridge. Continue around the edge, through a wicket gate to the man-made rampart built to protect the inhabitants from attackers coming across the top of the hill. Beyond the rampart is a lane.

$3\frac{1}{2}$ mile walk

Follow the lane back to Edge, a distance of about $1\frac{1}{2}$ miles, turning left at the T-junction after $\frac{1}{2}$ a mile.

To continue 4 or 6 mile walk

Although the next stretch is part of the Cotswold Way, the path is not at all clear. By the road is a signpost to Randwick and the path is down a steep bank into a field. In this field turn left and follow the wall along the side of the hill. Next there is a stile which leads into a rough pasture and woodland. Keep to the bottom edge of the woodland, at the foot of the scarp, and follow it for about 300 yards before the wood ends. At this point climb up the scarp onto the spur across which runs a deep rutted track. Turn left and follow the track for about 300 yards until it veers away to the left across the top of the hill. On the right, at this point, there is a bank (a fossilized field boundary) following the top of the south facing scarp. Follow this bank directly to Cripple Gate, 200 yards away, and the next signpost.

To continue 4 mile walk

Simply follow the lane back to Edge. This is the same lane as the $3\frac{1}{2}$ mile walk described above.

To continue 6 mile walk

At Cripple Gate the path to Randwick is clearly signposted through the deciduous plantation. It is about $1\frac{1}{4}$ miles and the only problem is a junction after 600 yards where the path divides into three. It is best to take the central path which brings you out on the Edge–Randwick lane opposite a radio mast, $\frac{1}{2}$ a mile above the main village of Randwick.

If you do not wish to return back along the scarp, simply follow the Edge lane. This is a 2 mile walk, $\frac{1}{2}$ a mile of which borders Painswick Common from where there is a good view of Painswick and its prominent church with its lean spire perched on the far slope.

Walk 8

Nympsfield—Uleybury—Uley
5½ miles

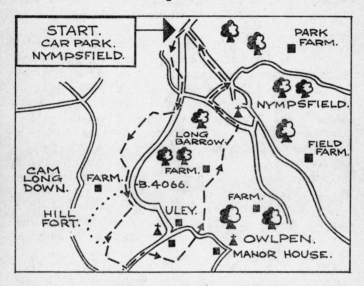

THIS is an energetic walk up and down the Cotswold scarp along the Cotswold Way to the great Iron Age fortress at Uleybury. After Uley it is up and down again but through very different country, via the combes that connect Uley to Nympsfield. Nympsfield is a fine example of a Cotswold village built almost entirely of local stone. The same stone doubtless as was used in the third millenium B.C. chambered tomb close by, where this walk begins. The top of the tomb was long ago removed, but the chambers in which 13 skeletons were found are in a fine state of preservation.

How to get there: The Nympsfield barrow is prominent by the side of the B4066, 6 miles south of Stroud.

By bus: The No. 415 from Stroud (bus station) to Berkeley

27

stops at the **Rose and Crown** in Nympsfield seven times a day.

Park in the very large car park by the Nympsfield chambered tomb.

Refreshments: The **Rose and Crown** in Nympsfield; there are several pubs, an hotel and confectioners in Uley.

The path begins by the barrow and is clearly signposted out along to Frocester Hill where there is a plan of this spectacular panorama. Continue along the hill for a further 200 yards, then follow the B4066 for about 300 yards before taking the signposted bridleway down through the deciduous woods in the direction of Uleybury. The path descends several hundred feet to the bottom of the scarp which it follows, and then opposite Cam Long Down (about $\frac{1}{4}$ of a mile on your right) it rises up the steep 400 yards to the north-east corner of the imposing 32 acre promontory fortress of Uleybury.

It does not matter which route you follow around the ramparts. However, at the south-east corner, the corner from where the village of Uley is clearly visible, take the path that leads down to the southern end of the High Street. The path is very clear, and when you reach the High Street turn left for about 100 yards. In the centre of the village on your right is South Street (next to a grocer's). Follow this lane for about $\frac{1}{2}$ a mile until it ends; at this point there is a stile and the path beyond it leads down across a stream and then northwards up a gentle slope towards a gate by a cottage underneath a prominent knoll. The distance from the stile to the cottage which is on the Uley–Owlpen lane is approximately 300 yards. By the cottage is a track which goes northwards for nearly a mile first skirting the bottom of the knoll, then up into a secluded combe. At the steep end of the combe is a hazel wood and the path goes straight on up through the wood and comes out on the top fields. Here the path is not clear, so continue straight on following the hedge and then the wall through two fields. You will arrive at the road directly behind the village of Nympsfield which you will see less than $\frac{1}{2}$ a mile away. Turn left along the road, then right after 400 yards into the village. To return to the Nympsfield barrow, take the Stroud road out of the village. This final stretch is about another $\frac{1}{2}$ mile.

Walk 9

Alderley—Tresham—Lower Kilcote
3½ and 5½ miles

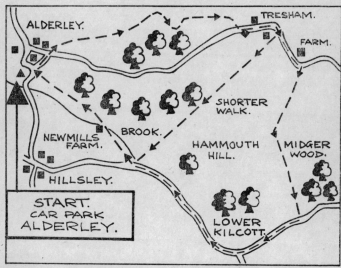

THIS is a stiff walk because these combes are now seldom walked, and the paths on the first stretch from Alderley to Tresham are overgrown. However, it is real Cotswold country and for that reason, and because it takes in the combes and the tops of the hills, it is a very pleasant walk. It also passes through the Midger Wood nature conservancy area where wildlife has been fostered for many years.

How to get there: Alderley is on a little lane tucked under the scarp 2 miles south of Wotton-under-Edge.

By bus: The No. 412 runs from Wotton-under-Edge to Hawkesbury Upton three times a day. There are services to Wotton-under-Edge from Stroud, Gloucester, and Bristol.

Refreshments: There is a confectioners in Tresham; in Wotton-under-Edge there are pubs and cafes.

Take the lane signposted to Tresham from the village, and by Gatehouse House on the edge of the village on your left is a lane that leads nearly a mile along the valley. It passes first a large modern cowshed, and then just past a row of derelict cottages on your right is the gate and footpath for Tresham. The path leads directly up to a small gate, and then on up to another. This second gate leads into a new plantation where the path has been partly obliterated. Keep to the east edge (on your left) of the plantation, and then bearing to your left in the next field climb up the steep slope, through a stile, which brings you puffing onto the top a few hundred yards behind the village of Tresham. The path up this slope is difficult, so pause and look for the stiles and gates when you are in doubt.

Turn left at the road near the village, and then walk on through the village, to a bridlepath on your right at the far end (signposted through a combe to Newmills and Alderley).

3½ mile walk

Follow the signposted path to Newmills. The section beyond Newmills is described at the end of the main walk.

To continue 5½ mile walk

Continuing past the bridlepath, the lane bends around the combe and there is a welcome confectioners on your right. After ½ a mile, on the bend just beyond Burden Court farm is a track which leads across the top to Midger Wood. The path is very clear down through this large wood; however, several paths cross our route so make sure you are descending and at the same time bearing to your right, and after about ½ a mile you will reach the lane near Lower Kilcote. Turn left and pass on through the hamlet in the direction of Alderley. After about a mile, and immediately after the second mill, take the track on your right (signposted). The path turns left after only a 100 yards and follows the brook to Newmills. From there climb up to the next field (on the side of the hill), and follow the hedgeline which becomes a track and leads into Alderley. It is an easy ¾ of a mile walk from Newmills to Alderley.

Walk 10

Old Sodbury—Horton—Little Kilcote
2½ and 4 miles

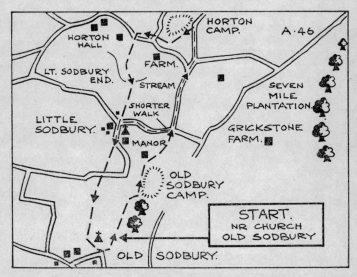

THIS is an easy walk along the Cotswold escarpment over-looking the Severn Vale. It includes two hillforts: Old Sodbury Camp, and Horton Camp which probably date to the first century B.C. Despite the imposing ramparts of Old Sodbury it was surrendered without a fight to the Romans, and in subsequent times its tranquility has only been disturbed by travellers and hill-walkers.

How to get there: Old Sodbury is on the A432, 2 miles east of Chipping Sodbury.

By bus: Take the No. 419 Bristol–Swindon bus; it stops in the village usually five times a day.

There is parking space by the village church situated immediately below the scarp.

Refreshments: There are several pubs and confectioners in the main village on the A432 about $\frac{1}{2}$ a mile from the church.

The path begins almost opposite the entrance to the church by the village school (signposted). It follows the bottom of the scarp for about $\frac{1}{2}$ a mile to a wood where it joins a bridleway. Go up through the wood, a distance of about 300 yards, and at the top bear left across to Little Sodbury Camp. Walk northwards (parallel to the scarp's face) through the interior of the fort and on the far side is a small wicket gate. You go through here and along the west wall of a barn to a track which leads through the farmyard and out into a field. Once you are in the centre of this field turn left in a northerly direction towards a stile prominent in the far wall which brings you out onto the Horton road.

$2\frac{1}{2}$ mile walk

Turn left here and walk down the hill to Little Sodbury church about $\frac{1}{2}$ a mile away. The return pathway to Old Sodbury from here is described at the end of the 4 mile walk.

To continue 4 mile walk

Take the lane for Horton ahead, and after $\frac{1}{2}$ a mile you will reach the fork for that village; however, fork right and after a further 50 yards fork left towards Hawkesbury; 300 yards on the left is a footpath, signposted, across the centre of the smaller Horton Camp and down into the village. There take the path (signposted) directly across the fields to Little Sodbury, keeping to the hedgeline on your right in the pasture after crossing a small stream. You will come out on the road into Little Sodbury. To return to Old Sodbury turn left past the church and go through the gate after the last house on your right, a distance of about $\frac{1}{4}$ of a mile. The path leads through this field to another road where you turn right for 20 yards then climb over the gate opposite and follow the hedgerows (for these are cultivated fields) three-quarters of a mile to Old Sodbury church. There is a turn-stile in the graveyard wall.

Walk 11

Chedworth—Chedworth Roman Villa—Withington Woods
3 and 5 miles

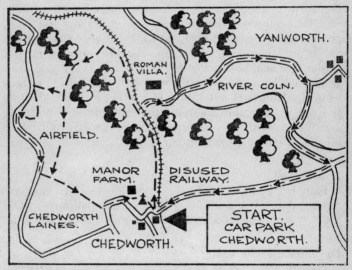

CHEDWORTH ROMAN VILLA is one of the largest and best preserved of its kind in Britain. This is an easy walk to the Villa from the village of Chedworth. The walk continues on and makes a large circle around the parish. The Villa is in the care of the National Trust; there is an entrance fee, an excellent guide-book by R. Goodburn and toilets and other facilities there.

How to get there: Chedworth village lies $7\frac{1}{2}$ miles north of Cirencester, a mile to the north-west of the A429.

By bus: Contact **Perrett & Son Ltd.,** Hill View, Shipton Oliffe for details.

Park in front of the church in the village.

Refreshments: There is the **Seven Tuns,** and several confectioners in Chedworth. There are also some refreshments on sale at the villa.

Set out from the **Seven Tuns** heading down into the village. Turn left after 50 yards by the post-box. The path begins after a further 40 yards on your right. Go over a stile and into the fields beyond a little allotment. Cross two fields keeping close to the disused railway on your right. The path continues up the slope before you, and is very clear on up through a copse and across the fields beyond to Chedworth Woods. The track through the woods to the villa is also very clear, and at strategic points there are signs. You arrive at the path which leads down to the right to the Villa, which is situated just beyond the woods.

3 mile walk

Instead of climbing back up to the path in the woods, continue along the lane from Chedworth in the direction of Yanworth. Just before the hamlet take the right-hand lane, and then after $\frac{1}{2}$ a mile you reach a T-junction. Turn right and soon you arrive back in Chedworth which nestles in the combe at the far side of the knoll from its famous Villa.

To continue 5 mile walk

Retrace your steps to the main path through the woods from which you turned off to visit the Villa. Once there continue straight on, as if you had not turned off. This path continues for about $\frac{3}{4}$ of a mile through the woods (be careful not to take any side tracks), and arrives at a surfaced lane beyond. (Keep relatively quiet through this stretch of the woods for it is a nature reserve.) Turn left up the road which climbs up through the woods and emerges at the disused airfield on the top. Here take the footpath along the north, woodland, edge of the airfield. On the far side is a track which follows the perimeter for about $\frac{1}{2}$ a mile before winding around to another road opposite Withington Woods. Many of the paths through these woods and the farmland on your right have been closed. However, the local councils may one day re-open them. For the present you must turn left along the road and follow it for $\frac{1}{4}$ of a mile and there turn left again in the direction of Chedworth. Before you turn off glance across the fields and if you are lucky you may see some deer—one of the attractions in re-opening the paths through that farmland. The $1\frac{1}{2}$ miles along the lane to Chedworth is quite clear. When you reach Manor farm on your left, go over the stile and down through the short avenue of beeches (in front of the farm). Beyond is a steep field full of mounds, vestiges of a medieval village, next to Chedworth church.

Walk 12

Daglingworth—the Duntisbournes—Winstone
5½ and 8 miles

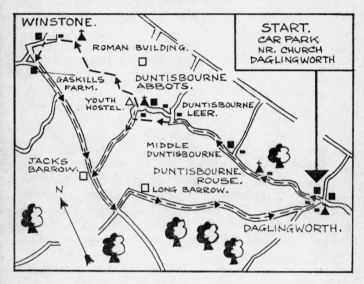

THIS is a walk around the lanes of the Duntisbourne valley and is recommended for those times of the year when the fields are wet and impassable. There are three very fine Saxon churches in the valley and the routes include these as well as the attractive later medieval church at Duntisbourne Abbots.

How to get there: Begin at Daglingworth which lies 5 miles north of Circencester just west of the A417.

By bus: The No. 422, Stroud–Cirencester bus stops five times a day at Daglingworth.
Parking: There is a large car park opposite the church at the south end of the village.

Refreshments: None, unfortunately, in the valley.

Begin at Daglingworth church. It has several Saxon windows including one made of re-used Roman tiles, and is famous for a series of tenth-eleventh century sculptures whose style is primitive.

Follow the lane northwards up the valley in the direction of Duntisbourne Rouse (signposted). It is a mile and a half to the next Saxon church which is on the right-hand side of the road just past the hamlet of Duntisbourne Rouse. It is one of the smallest and most picturesque churches in England, having a stone-tiled saddle-back tower. The fabric and quoining of the nave are Saxon in date; the chancel arch, the frescoes and chancel windows are early Norman. The chancel sits above a crypt, whilst out in the churchyard on the valley side is a fourteenth century cross.

Continue along the road northwards: after $\frac{1}{2}$ a mile you pass through the hamlet of Middle Duntisbourne; after a further mile you pass through Duntisbourne Leer. Duntisbourne Abbots, the largest settlement in the valley is another $\frac{1}{2}$ mile beyond the hamlet of Duntisbourne Leer. The church here also has a saddle-back tower, although its earliest features, the base of the tower and the nave aisles, are late twelfth century in date. The route from Daglingworth to this village is well-signposted and since the road is tucked into the side of the valley you are not exposed to the cold winter winds which can make walking on the hill-tops unpleasant.

$5\frac{1}{2}$ mile walk

If it is very cold and windy, you are advised to retrace your steps. However, an alternative route is as follows: Take the Edgeworth road out of Duntisbourne Abbots. This road is well signposted (to Sapperton as well as Edgeworth) at the top of the village, and runs to the left where the lane up out of Duntisbourne Abbots divides into three. Follow $\frac{3}{4}$ of a mile to the Jack Barrow crossroads. From here the remainder of the walk, to your left, is described in the last section of the main walk.

To continue 8 mile walk

The main walk continues to Winstone and part of it is across country. Although the path through the fields is a

38

relatively dry one it, nevertheless, can be wet at times.

Follow the footpath to Winstone (signposted) which is on the left of the lane leaving Duntisbourne Abbots in the direction of Birdlip, just beyond the Youth Hostel. It follows the dry Dunt valley, as it curves around, to a stile $\frac{1}{2}$ a mile from Duntisbourne Abbots. Beyond this valley is a track, and beyond this a large field. Keep the hedge on your right and keep straight on until you reach a small plantation after $\frac{1}{4}$ of a mile. The path follows the west edge of the plantation which will be on your right up another dry valley at the top of which is the Saxon church of Winstone.

This church has several Saxon features: the south doorway is crowned by a fine tympaneum; a blocked north doorway; an exceptionally large chancel arch and a splayed north-facing window. The church is situated $\frac{1}{4}$ of a mile to the east of the modern village. To get there follow the lane to your left. On your left, actually in the centre of the village, is a signposted path to Gaskill's farm, just across the fields on the Sapperton road which you must follow to your left. If, however, it is wet, continue through Winstone and at the T-junction beyond the village turn left. About $\frac{1}{2}$ a mile along this road are the remains of a round barrow at the rear of the elegant house on your right at Jack Barrow cross-roads.

Continue on for a further $\frac{1}{2}$ mile before turning left for Daglingworth. The road crosses the level fields, and after a sharp bend to your right a chambered long barrow is prominent on the left in the fields. If it is a clear day there is a fine view across the Cotswolds before you descend into Daglingworth.

Walk 13

Sapperton—Oakridge Lynch—Tunley
4 and 5½ miles

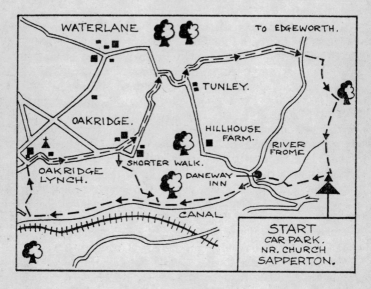

THIS walk follows the Thames and Severn canal for 2 miles from the famous Sapperton tunnel built between 1784 and 1789. The tunnel which is nearly 2 miles long is a marvellous feat of engineering now in a sadly decrepit state. It used to take the leggers, the men whose job it was to lie on their backs and propel the barges through the tunnel by pushing their legs against the roof, five hours to make the trip eastwards and three hours westwards. It is an easy walk along the tow-path and despite the steep climb to Oakridge Lynch the way along the lanes is easy as well. It is certainly a walk to be recommended when the fields are impassable.

How to get there: Sapperton lies a mile north of the A419 Cirencester–Stroud road, 6 miles from Cirencester.

By bus: The No. 422 Cirencester to Stroud bus stops at Sapperton five times a day.

Park by the church or by the curb in the centre of the village.

Refreshments: The **Bell Inn,** Sapperton; the **Daneway Inn,** en route, has a garden.

Begin at the church of St. Kenelm. Running down the side of the churchyard is a pathway which leads into the field beyond the church on the valley side. Turn left across the field descending only slightly to a stile in the hedge. Beyond the stile is the west entrance of the Sapperton tunnel over which you must go to the tow-path on the far side. Follow the tow-path for almost $\frac{1}{2}$ a mile to the **Daneway Inn** built in 1784 to lodge the tunnellers, and where the leggers later resided. From the Inn the tow-path is on the opposite side (signposted). For $\frac{1}{2}$ a mile there is a series of locks but once out of the woodland the canal becomes level.

Just before reaching the Oakridge Lynch road the railway comes into view on the left. Then there is a large mill-pond before a picturesque mill by the road. Turn left and then almost immediately right up the hillside to Oakridge Lynch. Almost at the crest of the hill the lane divides into three before the village green. On the edge of the green before you is a water trough with memorial plaques to those who died in World War I. One of these is most unusual; to Mabel Dearmer who died in 1915, aged 43, of fever on active service in Serbia. One of her relations also died far away at Gallipoli in the same year. Turn right at this junction to continue this walk. However, it is worth turning left just to visit the church $\frac{1}{4}$ of a mile along the road. Follow the lane to the right along the top of the hill to Oakridge $\frac{1}{2}$ a mile away.

4 mile walk

There is a five-ways at the beginning of the hamlet of Oakridge. Take the track on the right signposted to Iles Green which leads down the hillside to the canal. It rejoins the canal where it begins to climb, a mile or so from Sapperton church.

To continue 5½ mile walk

The main walk continues along the Edgeworth road forking left at the five-ways. The lane dips down through a beech wood and reaches a T-junction after ¾ of a mile. Turn right here for Tunley, a hamlet comprising a few attractive cottages, 50 yards down this lane. Turn left by the cottages and follow the lane up through the beech woods, and then across the top to the Daneway–Edgeworth road ¾ of a mile away. Go straight on along a track which has high hedges. After 40 yards the hedges end and the footpath back to Sapperton bears across the large field on your right to a gate into the far wood. When this field is sown it is best to skirt it to reach this gate. The path is direct downwards about ½ a mile to the stream, the River Frome; disregard the wood-cutters' tracks following the contours. From the Frome the path up to Sapperton church 400 yards away is steep but straightforward.

Walk 14

Slad—Bisley—Througham—The Camp
4, 6 and 9 miles

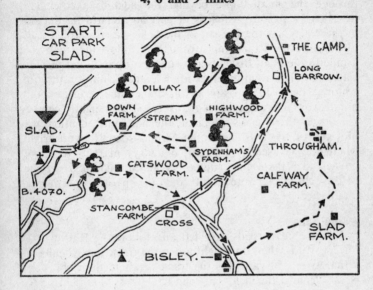

THESE walks are through marvellous variable countryside. The longest walk takes a good half day, passing through several hamlets, and finally following some of the loneliest valleys in the Cotswolds.

How to get there: Slad is on the B4070 3 miles north of Stroud.

By bus: The No. 563 from Cheltenham to Stroud stops at Slad six times a day.
Park on the verge or on the side of the lane which leaves the B4070 on the valley side in the centre of the village.

Refreshments: The **Woolpack** in Slad with a terraced garden; the **Stirrup Cup** and several confectioners in Bisley.

Take the Down farm lane on the valley side of the B4070

in the centre of the village. Follow it $\frac{1}{4}$ of a mile just past
Steambridge House. On your right is a track which crosses
the dam of an old mill-pond. The path continues from the
dam straight up the opposite field and then to the right up
through the small copse beyond the field to a stile. This
leads into a pasture which is in part an orchard on the side
of the valley. At the far end of the field is a stile which leads
through Furner's farm, and from there follow the track $\frac{1}{4}$ of
a mile to the Slad–Bisley road. Turn left up the road through
Catswood. The road emerges after a steep climb on the top;
continue on to the cross-roads at Stancombe farm almost a
mile away. At these cross-roads stood the eighth century
stone sculptured cross which in the nineteenth century was
moved a 150 yards down the Stroud road, to your right,
where it was used as a parish boundary marker. It was at
crosses like these that monks preached and held services
before churches were built and the parish system was
established.

4 mile walk

At these cross-roads turn left and follow the Birdlip road
for 200 yards, then turn right along the track for Sydenham's
farm. After 250 yards, as the track bends to the right, there
is a stile into the field on your left. Cross this field to the
next which descends down through medieval house-platforms
to a pathway by Sydenham's farm (to your right) perched on
the knoll overlooking a view which is one of the finest in the
Cotswolds. Follow the path downwards about $\frac{1}{2}$ a mile to a
cottage by a track which leads up to your right. This track
climbs up to Piedmont, in the woods, and from here the way
to the left is described in the main walk.

6 mile walk

At the Stancombe farm cross-roads turn left and follow the
Birdlip road until The Camp. From there the remainder of
the walk is described in the last section of the main walk.

To continue 9 mile walk

The main walk continues straight on to Bisley. After 200
yards fork left and you reach the centre of the village after

a further $\frac{1}{2}$ mile. Opposite the **Stirrup Cup** is a lane, marked 'No Through Road', which you must take. This becomes a track after 200 yards which leads down through the fields to a steep valley. Go straight down the valley side about 50 yards to a wicket gate the far side of a small stream. From there climb up the adjacent slope to a wicket gate on the side of the hill and a farm gate at the top of the slope. This leads onto a lane; go straight ahead, but bearing left, for about 50 yards and then on the bend is a stile on the right. The path leads across one field to another stile which leads into a large frequently cultivated field. The next stile is in the far right-hand corner of this field which at most times of the year you must skirt. Beyond this stile is a track which you take to the left and which leads to the hamlet of Througham $\frac{1}{2}$ a mile away. Here you reach a road where you go straight on, to the right, past a fine seventeenth century gabled house with pigeon lofts. Beyond this house fork left and after $\frac{1}{4}$ of a mile turn right. After a further $\frac{1}{2}$ a mile you reach the Stancombe farm cross-roads—The Camp road only a few hundred yards from The Camp. Just before the village on your left is a long barrow.

The path leaves this road in The Camp. It passes through the farmyard of the game-farm on the left in the village. Do not be deterred by this unexpected route but respect the fact that it is a farm. The path bears to the right after the yard and makes for a gate in the conifer wood on the right of the first field. The path continues for $\frac{1}{2}$ a mile down through this wood until a gate on the left at the head of the combe. The way is down the combe following the stream which flows down the centre of it to Dillay farm which is on your right. You cannot continue much further down the combe without a permit from the Gloucestershire Nature Conservancy for this is a reserve. Instead cross the stream and continue to a cottage tucked in a combe to your left. Behind the cottage is a bridlepath which is very clear and climbs up through the beech woods—a long steep climb to a track just below the summit of the hill. On the other side of this track 10 yards to your right is a stile into a field. The path is by the hedge and comes out at the picturesque late medieval farm of Sydenham. Turn right once over the stile by the farm and follow the track for 300 yards. At this point the track divides into three and you must take the left hand trackway down through the woods to Piedmont. Again the track divides into three, this time keep straight on. The path soon leaves the woods and goes down the valley side to the stream in the bottom and then up the opposite slope to Down farm. From here, to the left of the farm, is the lane which leads back past Steambridge House, where you began, to Slad $\frac{3}{4}$ of a mile away.

Walk 15

Great Badminton—Little Badminton—Luckington
4 and 6 miles

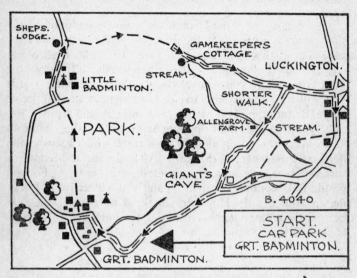

THIS walk is particularly recommended for those times of the year when the fields are muddy and impassable. It follows almost entirely the lanes and grass-tracks in and around the perimeter of Great Badminton Park. Be sure, however, if you have a dog, to control it in the Park where sheep regularly graze. Keep an eye out also for the famous Beaufort hunt based in Great Badminton.

How to get there: Badminton lies just north of the M4; turn off at the Dodington intersection. It lies 3½ miles east of the A46, and a mile north of the B4040.

By bus: Take the No. 419 Bristol–Swindon bus which stops in the village usually five times a day.
Park in the wide High Street.

Refreshments: There are pubs and confectioners in Great Badminton and Luckington.

What to see: Great Badminton House, and the grounds laid out by Capability Brown; 'Giant's Caves' chambered long barrow (published by J. X. Corcoran in the *Wiltshire Archaeological Magazine*, 65, 1970).

At the east end of the High Street in Great Badminton take the turning northwards in the direction of the Park. The Park gates lie on this road about 50 yards from the High Street (signposted). Follow the road (do not wander off) across the Park from where you will see the stately home. After a mile you will arrive at a lane and to your right is the hamlet of Little Badminton. Follow the lane through the hamlet and after $\frac{1}{2}$ a mile turn right opposite Shepherd's Lodge. After 40 yards keep straight on along a grass track which keeps to the northern perimeter of the Park. After a mile it becomes a surfaced lane once more by a game-keeper's cottage. For the 6 mile walk continue straight on and you will arrive at Luckington after a mile. However, for the 4 mile walk, $\frac{1}{2}$ a mile beyond the cottage there is a turning to your right, by a barn, back to Great Badminton.

4 mile walk

Turn right by the barn and follow the lane for nearly a mile to a T-junction. Turn right here and continue along the road which passes through the southern fringe of the park. Just before you turn right on this last occasion, there is a long barrow called Giant's Caves in a copse on the left of the road.

To continue 6 mile walk

Turn right in Luckington and follow the B4040 in the direction of Acton Turville almost to the edge of the village. Immediately before a row of council houses on the right is a stone stile. This path leads out into the fields behind the houses. You must bear south-eastwards through the fields (linked by gates), to a small stream. From here continue in the same direction a further $\frac{1}{2}$ mile down across a gentle slope to another stream. Immediately beyond it is the road, which if you turn right leads after $1\frac{1}{2}$ miles to **Great Badminton**. This is the road which the shorter walk joins, and which passes through the southern fringe of the **Park** for nearly a mile. The path from Luckington to the **Great Badminton** road is not well-marked. For the first section you should keep parallel to the B4040, but after the first stream you will lose sight of the road and so you must keep straight on. If it is wet, you are probably best advised to retrace your steps from Luckington in the Little Badminton direction, and at the barn fork left along the route described for the shorter walk.

Walk 16

Sherston—Westonbirt arboretum—Pinkney
5 and 6½ miles

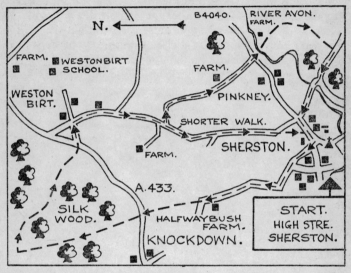

THIS is an easy walk from Sherston across the top to the famous arboretum at Westonbirt. It then returns down the lanes to Pinkney and crosses the park there.

How to get there: Sherston is a large village on the B4040, 6 miles west of Malmesbury.

By bus: Take the No. 419 Bristol–Swindon bus which stops at the **Angel Hotel** usually five times a day.

There is plenty of room to park in the High Street.

Refreshments: There are several pubs and confectioners in Sherston.

Take Church lane (at the Malmesbury end of the village) towards Knockdown. Just after Halfwaybush **(farm) nearly** a mile along this road there is a track on the right where the road bends sharply to the left. Follow this track about 600 yards to the A433. Go straight across the A433 and on into Silk Wood. This is a part of the Westonbirt arboretum, and many of the rarer species are labelled. Continue straight on for about a mile. Just before the woods end the path joins another following a valley to your right; this valley is currently a clearing. Follow this path, to your right, for about 300 yards to a gate which leads into the parkland (called the Downs) of Westonbirt House. If you wish to visit the arboretum proper, bear to the left up the slope and across the parkland. The main walk, however, keeps to the edge of Silk Wood and continues through the park for nearly a mile before reaching the A433.

Go straight across the main road, and turn right after 200 yards towards Sherston. The road to the left goes to Westonbirt village. After a further mile along this lane you reach a junction; the road to your left goes to Pinkney, but if you continue straight on you will arrive at Sherston.

5 mile walk

Continue towards Sherston for a mile. If ground conditions are dry, enter the village by a footpath that leaves the road after a left-hand bend. Actually on the bend is a signposted bridlepath to Knockdown. The path is on the right 40 yards beyond the signpost. The alternative is to simply follow the road to Sherston.

To continue 6½ mile walk

From the junction on the Westonbirt–Sherston road it is about a mile to Pinkney on the B4040. Cross directly over the B4040 to a track opposite which goes over the River Avon and past a large elegant farm on your left. After about a further ¼ of a mile the wall of Pinkney Park begins on your right. You follow this for 100 yards to a large ornamental gateway. The path goes through the gates and across the parkland, keeping straight ahead to a little lane, which if you turn right brings you back to Sherston.

Walk 17

Marshfield—Monkswood—St. Catherine's
4½ and 7 miles

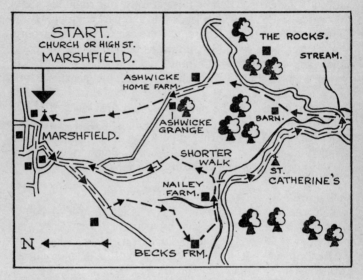

MARSHFIELD is now a sleepy town by-passed by a new Chippenham to Bristol road. Once it was a thriving halt on the London to Bristol road, and all the houses in the High Street are vestiges of those great coaching days. The country-side beyond is also very sleepy, and the footpaths around here are not easy-going. Local councils, however, are trying to signpost all the paths and make them passable. This is certain to make stretches of the walk described here a little easier. The particularly fine view of Bath from Ashwicke Home Farm makes it a memorable walk.

How to get there: Marshfield is on the A420 about 10 miles west of Chippenham.

By bus: Take the No. 335 Bristol–Chippenham bus which stops in the village around six times a day; or the No. 229

Bath–West Kington bus which stops around four time a day. Parking: Plenty of room in the High Street and around the church.

Refreshments: There are several Georgian period inns in Marshfield as well as confectioners. At St. Catherine's there are the Mead Tea Gardens.

Take the Colerne lane out of the High Street (signposted), and after ¼ of a mile turn right for Beck's Farm. After a further ½ a mile take a bridlepath with high hedges on your left. Go along this for only 150 yards until the path bends and on the right is a gate. Go over the gate and along the side of the combe and down towards Beck's Farm following the hedgerow. Walk past the first farm-cottages (on your left), and enter a yard beyond which is a large barn. On your left is a stile and the path that leads westwards down the valley. However, this path is not very clear so do not descend to the brook visible in the valley bottom until you have left the first field directly below those farm-cottages. After following the brook for about 500 yards you reach the Marshfield–St. Catherine's lane.

4½ mile walk

If you need refreshment, follow the directions for the 7 mile walk as far as the Mead Tea gardens in St. Catherine's, and then retrace your steps to the point where the Marshfield–St. Catherine's lane crosses the brook, as just described, and from there continue up the hill to Marshfield. This lane is seldom used by vehicles.

To continue 7 mile walk

Turn right along the lane and after 40 yards at a T-junction turn left to St. Catherine's. The village, its elegant court and church are about ½ a mile from this last junction. The tea gardens are at the far end of the village. Shortly after the gardens is another road back to Marshfield on the left. Take this lane and after crossing a stream, a matter of about 50 yards from the turn-off, take the path (signposted) along the valley to your left. There are stiles in and out of the first two fields, and at the beginning of the third. The path then joins

53

a track in the third field which bears to the left then up to a barn prominent on the hillside. The path to Marshfield continues to the right of the barn, directly along the side of the hill, rejoining the road in a plantation about $\frac{1}{2}$ a mile beyond the barn. (There are no stiles, as yet, out of this field. The council is erecting some stiles, but you may prefer in the meantime to follow the lane which runs parallel to the path just described); 100 yards along this lane is the path (signposted) to Ashwicke Home Farm. Follow this track up the valley; after 400 yards it turns right and winds up through the woods to a pasture. There is a good path through this field to the farm on the top. From the farm follow the road in the Marshfield direction (to your left), for about 400 yards. On a sharp left-hand bend there is a path signposted to Marshfield through the fields. The path is clear for the first two fields. In the third field keep to the right of the hedge, and once over the crest of a small hill Marshfield and its church come into view. Follow the path, which is very clear, for about $\frac{3}{4}$ of a mile, to Marshfield.

Walk 18

Colerne—Middlehill—Box—Widdenham
4, 5 and 6 miles

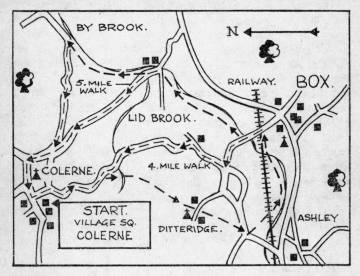

THIS is a very varied walk through several valleys in the southern fringes of the Cotswolds. In fact, most of it is through the large parish of Box, and it passes close to the famous tunnel built for the Great Western Railway by Brunel. For nearly 3 miles the walk follows the meandering By Brook; those who have all day and enjoy these few miles can follow the brook all the way to Castle Combe by linking the sections of this walk, with sections of walks 19 and 20.

How to get there: Colerne is 5 miles north of Bath, just east of the Fosse Way.

By bus: Take the No. 230 Bath–Colerne bus which usually runs ten times a day.

There is parking space in the little village square at the north end of the High Street by the church.

Refreshments: Lord Nelson (Colerne); several pubs in Box; confectioners in both villages.

What to see: Ditteridge church (eleventh century); Box tunnel.

Opposite the **Lord Nelson** in Colerne High Street is the steep lane which is signposted to Box. Walk down this small twisting road (from where there are excellent views of the By Brook valley) about 400 yards until it straightens out slightly. At this point, on the right, is a metal stile into a small field. Follow the hedgerow until the end of the field and there turn **right** bearing down across the slope about 40 yards to the Lid Brook across which is a wooden footbridge. The bridge is concealed in the hawthorns protecting the stream, and the path is not always clear, so if in doubt after leaving the first field make for the brook and follow it up-stream. Beyond the bridge is a fence-line which goes straight up the side of the valley; follow the left side of this fence and after two stiles you will arrive (puffing) at the top of the valley. Turn left then and after 20 yards follow the right side (or whichever side is not being cultivated) of another fence across the hill-top. There is a splendid view by the elm on the top of the hill, in all directions.

By following this fence you arrive at the lane that leads into Ditteridge, and in fact passes the charming early Norman church in the village. The lane brings you to the war-memorial cross and a road junction. Turn left and then almost immediately on the right is a stile which leads down through a pasture to a row of cottages. These were built to accommodate the employees of the adjacent Spa House when Middlehill experienced a twenty year boom in tourists on discovering that there were hot springs beneath the hamlet. Unfortunately, for Middlehill, Beau Nash's fame in Bath attracted most of the takers of the hot waters away to that thriving centre, and Middlehill's prominence was short-lived. Continue past these cottages and on down the track about 200 yards to the five ways. Three of these ways are surfaced lanes, the fourth directly opposite is the footpath to Box (signposted) which follows By Brook. Next to the signpost is a cottage and a stile; this leads through a field, on through a tunnel beneath the railway and into the meadows by the brook. Simply follow the brook until after 1000 yards you reach a footbridge. At this point **if you want to see Box tunnel** you should turn left and climb up the hillside to the left of the small copse. From the top of the copse there is an excellent view of Brunel's tunnel built between 1836 and 1841 at the cost of more than a hundred lives. Also at the bridge, if you wish to visit Box, you should cross over and follow the path and the subsequent lane up to the village where there are several pubs about $\frac{1}{2}$ a mile away.

Continuing from this bridge, follow the left bank of the brook to the end of the meadow where there is a stile, then follow a footpath for about 200 yards to Mill Lane. Turn left here, go under the railway bridge and on for another 100 yards to the main entrance of Spafax.

4 mile walk

At this point, continue along the lane for another $\frac{1}{2}$ mile. It winds up the hillside and just past a farm on your right is a turning to Colerne. Take this for 400 yards and then fork left opposite two farm-cottages. This is in fact the lane on which you set out from Colerne. From these farm-cottages to the **Lord Nelson** it is just over one mile.

To continue 5 and 6 mile walks

There is a stile at the main entrance to Spafax, and the path follows the right bank of the brook until a weir where it crosses to the left bank. The path continues through two peaceful meadows. Leave the second of these by the gate which leads into the edge of a higher field; 40 yards beyond you is a stile in the fence onto a small lane. Turn right down the lane, and after 40 yards turn left in the direction of Colerne.

5 mile walk

From this point simply follow the lane as it climbs the hillside back up to the market place at Colerne.

To continue 6 mile walk

If you want to savour a little more of these peaceful meadows you should take the path which begins opposite Salt Box farm, 50 yards from the last junction. The brook is very slow here and it is a favourite haunt of herons. Follow the path over three meadows when you will arrive at the Colerne–Widdenham lane. Here you should turn left, up the lane a mile or so, back to Colerne and its imposing church.

Walk 19

Rudloe Manor—Biddestone—Slaughterford—Weavern
5 miles

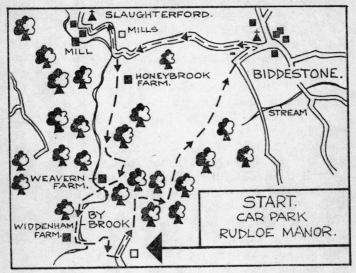

THIS is an easy walk which follows the old road from Rudloe manor to Biddestone and then returns via Slaughterford along the By Brook. It is particularly recommended as an autumnal walk for it passes through some fine beech woods, and the way is frequently lined by blackberry bushes.

How to get there: Rudloe manor is $\frac{1}{2}$ a mile to the north of the A4 on the Chippenham side of Box. The lane is actually on a sharp bend in the A4, and is signposted.

By bus: Take the No. 465 Bath–Chippenham bus which runs every 45 minutes, and stops opposite the lane to Rudloe manor, on the A4.

There is limited parking along this lane, so park close to the hedgerow where other vehicles can pass, although there is very little traffic along here.

Refreshments: There is a pub in Biddestone.

From the manor (H.Q., R.A.F. Rudloe) follow the lane to its end, a distance of 400 yards. There climb over a gate and follow the edge of the field straight on for a further 400 yards to a plantation. There is a track down through this wood. Fork right after 50 yards then descend the hill to the valley and climb back up the opposite hill. The track keeps straight on until the plantation ends after a further $\frac{1}{2}$ a mile and you reach the Weavern farm–Biddestone lane. Turn right and follow the hedged lane to Biddestone $1\frac{1}{2}$ miles away. Biddestone has been voted the best kept village in England, and has a particularly attractive green beyond which lies the pub. The lane which leads into the village first meets the Hartham Park road on your right, and then after 50 yards the Slaughterford road on your left. Take this road towards Slaughterford which crosses the top fields, then after a mile descends towards By Brook. On a steep right-hand bend as the road enters a wood, there is a track on your left. This is the path to Weavern farm.

However, you may wish to walk a further $\frac{1}{2}$ mile into Slaughterford, which was supposedly named after the Danes had been massacred by the Saxons here. There is a large paper-mill on your left, a picturesque bridge and a little church at the far end of the village which stands alone in a field.

To continue the walk follow the Weavern track through the woods for nearly a mile. The track runs parallel to the brook though well above it for most of the way, then it bends to the left away from the brook and you leave the trees. After a further 50 yards there is a stile on your right (where the track meets the gravelled lane). The path now follows the hedgerow down through a field towards the brook. In the next field it bends to your right towards Weavern farm, a derelict mill. You do not actually go to the farm but strike out to a bridge which crosses the brook 50 yards on your left. From this bridge follow the brook as it meanders through two long meadows to Widdenham farm, which was also once a mill. There is a lane by the farm where you turn left, and re-cross the brook. At the foot of the valley side, just beyond the brook, the lane becomes a bridlepath and climbs up between high hedges to Rudloe manor perched on the top.

Walk 20

Castle Combe—Nettleton Mill—Long Dean
3 and 5½ miles

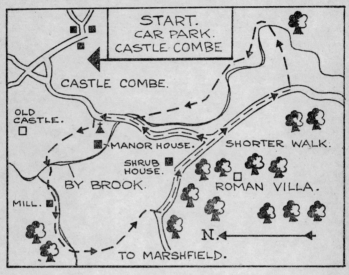

CASTLE COMBE has been called Britain's most beautiful village. It is certainly very attractive for many of the fifteenth century weavers' cottages, built by Sir John Fastolf with money he made in the French wars, are still surviving. It is difficult to believe that in the fifteenth century Castle Combe was one of the foremost industrial centres in England. There are slightly more recent mills, which are no longer operative, in the hamlets of Nettleton and Long Dean through which this walk passes.

How to get there: Castle Combe lies about 6 miles north-west of Chippenham, just off the B4039.

By bus: Take the No. 291 Chippenham-Sherston bus which stops seven times a day in the village.

Parking: There is limited space in the village; however, near the B4039 is a large car park (signposted).

Refreshments: There are several pubs, tea-shops and confectioners in Castle Combe.

Take the lane off the High Street which leads behind the fourteenth century market cross. Almost immediately turn right under an archway and follow the path up the hill to a stile about 200 yards away. From here the path skirts the left-hand side of the top field (signposted), and then descends down to a bridge over the By Brook, 400 yards from the stile. Go across the bridge and then follow the track to your right which runs parallel to the brook through several fields and on to Nettleton mill. The mill is now derelict but it is in reasonable condition and is therefore quite an interesting monument. The path is to your left between the mill and the barn. It follows a track up through deciduous woods to a clapper bridge across a tributary of By Brook. Go over the bridge and on up the footpath for about $\frac{1}{2}$ a mile until it meets a road, the North Wraxall–Ford lane. Turn left along the road (in the direction of Ford), and after $\frac{1}{2}$ a mile you come to a T-junction.

3 mile walk

At this T-junction turn left following the lane down through the woods to Castle Combe. In the summer this lane can be busy so be careful.

To continue 5½ mile walk

The main walk continues to the right at the T-junction. Follow the lane for $\frac{1}{2}$ a mile and then, just before you reach the beech woods, you enter the field on your left. The path goes down the sloping field towards a far corner of the field where there is a gate. From where you enter the field the gate is just visible, set in the fence on the edge of the woods which cling to the valley side. The path, an old lane, descends down through the woods to the secluded hamlet of Long Dean. Turn left in the hamlet almost immediately you have crossed the brook and follow the track up the hillside past a mill on your left. It climbs 400 yards to a stone stile in woods on the top. From there the path is clear, following the top of the valley above the brook for about $\frac{1}{2}$ a mile. It then slowly descends into the valley. You arrive eventually at a stone bridge across the brook at the edge of Castle Combe which is to your right.